From Europe to Outside:
A Brief of History in Law

by

Prof. Manuel Freire-Garabal y Núñez

(Phd. H., MBA., LLB.)

**Associate Professor of Asean
University International**

Dedicated to my beloved father, a true piece of alive History

About the author

Prof. Sir Manuel Freire-Garabal y Núñez Phd. H., MBA., LLB (Santiago de Compostela, 1995) is a Spanish jurist, diplomat, journalist and academic.

He is Graduated in Law in A Coruña University (2013-2017), Graduated in Journalism at National Journalists Association of Cuba in Exile (2013-2017) and MBA in "International Construction Management" at European University of Madrid (2017-2018).

He made different specializations in business, management and cybersecurity at Wharton University, INSEAD Business School, New York University, Berklee Music, Columbia University, University of Los Andes, University of Colorado and at Yonsei University.

He also realized courses at universities and business schools as ESSEC Business School, Harvard University, Indian School of Business, London Business School, Saudi Electronic University, Stanford University, The Johns Hopkins University, University of Washington, Vanderbilt University and Yale University.

He received in 2019 the Honorary Doctorate (*Honoris Causa*) in Human Rights and Diplomacy by the Asean University International (Indonesia) and Honorary Doctorate of Philosophy in Enviromental Peace by Noble International University (USA).

In 2016 he started in the field of Law research about family law and private property. Since his beginnings in the academic field he became member of several national and international academies and received more than twenty National and International awards.

Sir Manuel is advisor of some Princes and Royal Houses around the World as well as Honorary Ambassador of different organisations related to United Nations.

Since July of 2018 he is the President of the Private Council of the Prince Mahmoud Salah Al Din Assaf of Saudi Arabia.

Since 2019, he is contributor of Le Monde and Le Figaro, two of the best 25 newspapers of the World.

He has been featured as author and entrepreneur in media like Cosmo, CNBC, CBS, ABC and Fox News.

Is considered of one of the Most Influent by different journals and magazines as *UpClosed* or *Mundo Extremo*. Since 2018 is considered one of the Most Influent Men in the Middle East since he received the

© *Prof. Manuel Freire-Garabal y Núñez*

award "Best Human Leader in the World for 2017".

In 2019, the magazine Cosmo Chic made a special review about his position between the 250 Top Influencersof Middle East of 2019. In the same year was included as Honorary member "World Order of Global Leaders" and also Nominee to the award "The Face of the Globe in Service to Humanity 2019" given by Global Public Excellence with support of Nelson Mandela Foundation.

He is works in Higher Education in university as Associate Professor and Vicepresident of Communications at Asean University International as advisor of IIC University and of City University Group and as invited contributor about Higher Education in the Official blog of News of Harvard University in, MSNBC and Microsoft Education.

© *Prof. Manuel Freire-Garabal y Núñez*

About Asean University International

AUI (Asean University International) has been the leading innovator of flexible study for over 5 years because we're committed to helping busy adults study from anywhere.

Global universities, colleges and students leading delivery of the UN Sustainable Development Goals' calls on the UN to better promote the role of higher and further education in all of the SDGs rather than only Goal 4 and on senior management in universities and colleges to look for innovative ways to increase staff and student capacity to address the SDGs.

Asean University International is a contributing institution to a Global Alliance of the world's universities, colleges and sustainability networks have today (Wednesday, 11th July) launched a new report; 'Global universities, colleges and students leading delivery of the UN Sustainable Development Goals'. Presented at the UN High Level Political Forum in New York, the research calls on the UN to better promote the role of higher and further education in all of the SDGs rather than only Goal 4 and on senior management in universities and colleges to look for innovative ways to increase staff and student capacity to address the SDGs.

© *Prof. Manuel Freire-Garabal y Núñez*

Disclaimer

The information contained in this eBook is offered for informational purposes solely, and it is geared towards providing exact and reliable information in regards to the topic and issue covered. The author and the publisher does not warrant that the information contained in this e-book is fully complete and shall not be responsible for any errors or omissions.

The author and publisher shall have neither liability nor responsibility to any person or entity concerning any reparation, damages, or monetary loss caused or alleged to be caused directly or indirectly by this e-book. Therefore, this eBook should be used as a guide - not as the ultimate source.

The publication is sold with the idea that the publisher is not required to render accounting, officially permitted, or otherwise, qualified services. If advice is necessary, legal or professional, a practiced individual in the profession should be ordered.

In no way is it legal to reproduce, duplicate, or transmit any part of this document in either electronic means or printed format. Recording of this publication is strictly prohibited, and any storage of this document is not allowed unless with written permission from the publisher. All rights reserved.

The author own all copyrights not held by the publisher. The trademarks that are used are without any consent, and the publication of the trademark is without permission or backing by the trademark owner. All trademarks and brands within this book are for clarifying purposes only and are not affiliated with this document.

Table of Content

Introduction

Europe is a large continent with numerous different countries that has a lot to offer. It has been known for many notable places and buildings, such as the Eiffel Tower in Paris, the leaning tower of Pisa in Italy, etc.

Today's European legal order, with the European Court of Justice (ECJ) at its centre, provides the authoritative settlement of disputes between states, European institutions, firms and individuals within the European Union (EU).

Particularly when compared to other treaty-based dispute settlement systems, the EU's legal system is recognized as remarkably effective, intrusive and innovative.

The European legal order has, indeed, come a long way since Article 164 of the 1958 Treaty of Rome provided for a Court of Justice 'to ensure

© *Prof. Manuel Freire-Garabal y Núñez*

that in the interpretation and application of this Treaty the law is observed'.

The strength of the European legal order is often understood to derive from a set of 'revolutionary' doctrines first established by the Court of Justice in 1963 and 1964.

These doctrines, most prominently the direct effect and supremacy of European law, but also the comprehensive rejection of self-help enforcement by the European states, distinguished the then emerging European legal order from general international law and provided for private individuals and domestic courts to take a direct role in enforcing European obligations within their national legal orders.

Over time, as these doctrines were extended to a wider range of scenarios and as they came to be understood and accepted (not without hesitations) by policymakers, courts and private actors within the European states, these early decisions of the Court provided the foundations of European law as we now know it.

In preparing this outline of the brief history of in law of Europe, from the earliest beginnings of civilization down to the present, those topics have been chosen which have the greatest interest for us today - those which help us most in understanding our own time.

© *Prof. Manuel Freire-Garabal y Núñez*

Roman Law

Roman law was the law of the city of Rome and subsequently of the whole Roman Empire. The development of Roman law comprises more than a thousand years of jurisprudence which developed in different phases.

A highwatermark in Roman jurisprudence was the Corpus Juris Civilis (AD 529-34) prepared under the direct guidance of Emperor Justinian. The Corpus Iuris Civilis is a remarkable legacy from a remarkable era in legal history.

Five and a half centuries after Justinian, the 'jurisprudence' of Rome was studied in the universities of Northern Italy. Nicholas, in his book, An Introduction to Roman Law, noted that this phase of Roman law gave to almost the whole of Europe a common stock of legal ideas, a common grammar of legal thought and, to a varying but considerable extent, a common mass of legal rules.'

Nicholas observed that England stood out against the 'reception' of Roman law and retained its own Common law – but that the Common law too has been, in part, influenced by Roman law.

Today, there are two great legal systems of European origin – the Common law of England (influenced to a small extent only by Roman law) and the Civil law shaped largely by the revived Roman law. The Common law is the basis of the legal systems of most English-speaking nations.

The Civil law is the basis of the legal systems of countries of the continent of Europe and countries in South America and elsewhere. The other great non-European legal systems, the Hindu and the Mohammedan, are largely religious based but have 'imported' aspects of the Common law and Civil law into commercial transactions.

Students of law will be familiar with the concepts of, and distinctions between, public law and private law. Public law relates to the regulation of the state; constitutional law is described as a branch of public law.

Private law regulates legal relationships among individuals and the greatest influence of Roman law has been in the sphere of private law and this paper is confined to this aspect of law.

Phases Of Roman History

A significant phase of Roman history ended in 510 BC with the expulsion of King Tar□uinius Superbus. From then the Roman Republic developed as a small city-state.

By 272 BC, following a period of territorial expansion, Rome's control over Italy was almost complete.

In two wars 264-241 BC, 218-201 BC Carthage, a rival for the Central Western Mediterranean, was eventually defeated. Subsequently Rome was at war with the East. Territorial expansion in the second century BC changed the face of Italy from small farming holdings to large estates with slave labour.

Over a period, a professional army became mobilised. This enhanced the power of ambitious generals setting a pattern.

After much strife, a period of peace and stability commenced in 27 BC and Octavian, known as Augustus, restored constitutional government and the Empire took shape.

The history of the Empire is often divided into two periods, the Principate (27 BC –AD 284) and that of the Dominate or absolute monarchy which followed.

© *Prof. Manuel Freire-Garabal y Núñez*

Sources And Forms Of Roman Law

In terms of sources of written law, the Twelve Tables (c. 451 BC) were both a 'statute' (lex) and a code. The pronouncements of the Emperor had the force of law (lex). "Magisterial" law developed from the edicts of the magistrates and above all from the Urban Praetor.

The day-to-day functions of the Praetor were to grant remedies in individual cases.

Today, in the common law world, the interpretation of the law in a binding form in disputes is within the jurisdiction of the courts with professional judges. Nicholas wrote that in Rome in the formative period of the law there were no professional judges and no regular courts; the interpretation of the law was discharged by the priestly "college of pontifices" and subsecuently by lay jurists. When the period of the Dominate emerged, the sole source of law became the Emperor.

Justin, an elderly soldier, born of a peasant family in what became Yugoslavia, came to the throne in 518 AD. His nephew and adopted son was Justinian who received the best education available in Constantinople.

Justinian acceded to the throne in 527 AD. He ordered his chief jurists to extract the best and most reliable sections of the earlier Roman texts for inclusion under appropriate headings in a Digest.

All prior texts were to be destroyed throughout the Empire with the purpose of eliminating error. The Digest was ready by 533 AD.

Justinian also directed his jurists to prepare a textbook for law students called Justinian's Institutes which was completed by 533 AD. The following year Justinian's jurists completed a final version of all the Imperial statutes known as the Codex.

The texts known at the Digest, the Institutes and the Codex became generally known as the Corpus Juris Civilis, the "body of law". Subsecuently the law of Justinian became the bedrock of the law of the continent of Europe.

Roman law enjoyed a renewal during the renaissance of learning at the end of the eleventh century.

The great teacher Irnerius (c.1055-c. 1130) who taught at Bologna expounded the Corpus Juris Civilis text by text. Irnerius and his successors became known as the "Glossators". Roman law became a popular subject of study at the universities of Italy.

The Institutes became one of the most read law books of all time and was significantly influential. Law students in many countries are required to read the Institutes to the present day.

24

I set down here an extract from the Institutes translated by Thomas Collett Sandars   which demonstrates   a remarkable   elegance of expression and nobility of thought:

"Liber Primus: Tit.1. De Justitia et Jure: Justice is the constant and perpetual wish to render everyone his due.

1. Jurisprudence is the knowledge of things divine and human: the science of the just and the unjust.

2. Having explained these general terms, we think we shall commence our exposition of the law of the Roman people most advantageously, if our explanation is at first plain and easy, and is then carried on into details with the utmost care and exactness.

For, if at the outset we overload the mind of the student, while yet new to the subject and unable to bear much, with a multitude and variety of topics, one of two things will happen – we shall either cause him wholly to abandon his studies, or, after great toil, and often after great distrust of himself (the most frequent stumbling block in the way of youth), we shall at least conduct him to the point, to which, if he had been led by a smoother road, he might, without great labour, and without any distrust of his own powers, have been sooner conducted.

3. The maxims of the laws are these: to live honestly, to hurt no one, to give everyone his due..."

Leaving aside the noble ideas expressed in the Institutes the paternal care of the Emperor for law students is so very "modern".

In Roman jurisprudence, there were three different kinds of ius. Ius naturale was the law of nature. It included everything beyond the power of human law- making. The idea of 'natural law' developed from the ius naturale and included the concept of fundamental human rights inherent in man which cannot be taken away by human law.

The writings of Cicero (106-43 BC), (court advocate and politician before the Christian era) influenced the development of the ius naturale which in turn have influenced the natural-law doctrines of the medieval Roman Catholic Church and what have been described as 'secularised' natural-law theories. In his De Legibus, Cicero wrote:

"True law is right reason in agreement with nature, diffused among all men; constant and unchanging, it should call men to their duties by its precepts, and deter them from wrongdoing by its prohibitions...

To curtail this law is unholy, to amend it illicit, to repeal it impossible; nor can we be dispensed from it by the order either of the senate or of popular assembly; nor need we look for anyone to clarify or interpret it; nor will it be one law at Rome and a different law at Athens, nor otherwise tomorrow than it is today; but one and the same law, eternal and unchangeable, will bind all peoples and all ages; and God its designer, expounder and enacter, will be as it were the sole and universal ruler and governor of all things;..."

Another ius was the ius civile, the body of laws that applied originally to Roman citizens and the Praetores Urbani – those who had jurisdiction over cases involving citizens.

The term "civil law" in the sense of Roman-based legal doctrine comes from ius civile. This is what we would designate as "positive law" today.

In the Institutes, it is written: "Every community governed by laws and customs uses partly its own law, (the civil law – the law of the particular state) and partly laws common to all mankind".

There were further distinctions between 'written' laws referred to as leges or lex and the Roman concept of equitas from where the term "equity" is derived – the doing of justice in a given factual circumstance ameliorating perhaps the harsh effect of a written law.

Ius gentium referred to the law of nations. These were human-made laws but "common to all mankind".

Today we would designate ius gentium as "international law". Rules of diplomacy and state relations were governed by the ius gentium.

Laws relating to commercial trade and commercial practices were also comprised in the ius gentium – what we call "private international law" today. Modern international

© *Prof. Manuel Freire-Garabal y Núñez*

law including admiralty law has been significantly influenced by this aspect of Roman law.

The Roman law of "things" ("res") - economic assets - was divided into the law of property ('things' in a restricted sense), the law of succession and the law of obligations. Today this division of the law is a cardinal feature of the modern Civil law.

The law of sale is set out in Justinian's Institutes (Tit. XX11 De Consensu Obligatione). The Romans were great merchants – men of business - and built a business empire which re□uired law to regulate their transactions. This extract below refers to the law of obligations:

"Obligations are formed by the mere consent of the parties in the contracts for sale, of letting to hire, of partnership, and of mandate. An obligation is, in these cases, said to be made by the mere consent of the parties; because there is no necessity for any writing, nor even for the presence of the parties; nor is it requisite that anything should be given to make the contract binding, but the mere consent of those between who the transaction is carried on suffices."

Legacies Of Roman Law

Roman law has left many legacies. The Emperor Justinian, building on earlier jurists, codified in a structured written form a sophisticated system of law by means of the Digest, Codex and the Institutes. This codified system of law has influenced much of the Civil law world.

The concepts inherent in the legal order comprised in the ius naturale and ius gentium, intended to extend beyond national border, are today the cornerstones of human rights law and international law throughout the world.

© Prof. Manuel Freire-Garabal y Núñez

With the Romans, law developed into a science and we write today of the science of the law.

The Early Middle Ages

People use the phrase "Middle Ages" to describe Europe between the fall of Rome in 476 CE and the beginning of the Renaissance in the 14th century.

Many scholars call the era the "medieval period" instead; "Middle Ages," they say, incorrectly implies that the period is an insignificant blip sandwiched between two much more important epochs.

The phrase "Middle Ages" tells us more about the Renaissance that followed it than it does about the era itself.

Starting around the 14th century, European thinkers, writers and artists began to look back and celebrate the art and culture of ancient Greece and Rome.

Accordingly, they dismissed the period after the fall of Rome as a "Middle" or even "Dark" age in which no scientific accomplishments had been made, no great art produced, no great leaders born.

The people of the Middle Ages had squandered the advancements of their predecessors, this argument went, and mired themselves instead in what 18th-century English historian Edward Gibbon called "barbarism and religion."

Did you know? Between 1347 and 1350, a mysterious disease known as the "Black Death" (the bubonic plague) killed some 20 million people in Europe — 30 percent of the continent's population. It was especially deadly in cities, where it was impossible to prevent the transmission of the disease from one person to another.

This way of thinking about the era in the "middle" of the fall of Rome and the rise of the Renaissance prevailed until relatively recently.

However, today's scholars note that the era was as complex and vibrant as any other.

The Catholic Church

After the fall of Rome, no single state or government united the people who lived on the European continent. Instead, the Catholic Church became the most powerful institution of the medieval period. Kings, Queens and other leaders derived much of their power from their alliances with and protection of the Church.

(In 800 CE, for example, Pope Leo III named the Frankish king Charlemagne the "Emperor of the Romans"– the first since that empire's fall more than 300 years before. Over time, Charlemagne's realm became the Holy Roman Empire, one of several political entities in

Europe whose interests tended to align with those of the Church.)

Ordinary people across Europe had to "tithe" 10 percent of their earnings each year to the Church; at the same time, the Church was mostly exempt from taxation. These policies helped it to amass a great deal of money and power.

The Rise Of Islam

Meanwhile, the Islamic world was growing larger and more powerful. After the prophet Muhammad's death in 632 CE, Muslim armies conquered large parts of the Middle East, uniting them under the rule of a single caliph. At its height, the medieval Islamic world was more than three times bigger than all of Christendom.

Under the caliphs, great cities such as Cairo, Baghdad and Damascus fostered a vibrant intellectual and cultural life. Poets, scientists and philosophers wrote thousands of books (on paper, a Chinese invention that had made its way into the Islamic world by the 8th century).

Scholars translated Greek, Iranian and Indian texts into Arabic.

Inventors devised technologies like the pinhole camera, soap, windmills, surgical instruments, an early flying machine and the system of numerals that we use today. And religious scholars and mystics translated, interpreted and taught the Quran and other scriptural texts to people across the Middle East.

The Crusades

Toward the end of the 11th century, the Catholic Church began to authorize military expeditions, or Crusades, to expel Muslim "infidels" from the Holy Land.

Crusaders, who wore red crosses on their coats to advertise their status, believed that their service would guarantee the remission of their sins and ensure that they could spend all eternity in Heaven. (They also received more worldly rewards, such as papal protection of their property and forgiveness of some kinds of loan payments.)

The Crusades began in 1095, when Pope Urban summoned a Christian army to fight its way to Jerusalem, and continued on and off until the end of the 15th century. No one "won" the Crusades; in fact, many thousands of people from both sides lost their lives. They did make ordinary Catholics across Christendom feel like they had a common purpose, and they inspired waves of religious enthusiasm among people who might otherwise have felt alienated from the official Church.

They also exposed Crusaders to Islamic literature, science and technology–exposure that would have a lasting effect on European intellectual life.

Art And Architecture

Another way to show devotion to the Church was to build grand cathedrals and other ecclesiastical structures such as monasteries.

Cathedrals were the largest buildings in medieval Europe, and they could be found at the center of towns and cities across the continent.

Between the 10th and 13th centuries, most European cathedrals were built in the Romanesque style. Romaneque cathedrals are solid and substantial: They have rounded masonry arches and barrel vaults supporting the roof, thick stone walls and few windows.

© *Prof. Manuel Freire-Garabal y Núñez*

(Examples of Romanesque architecture include the Porto Cathedral in Portugal and the Speyer Cathedral in present-day Germany.)

Around 1200, church builders began to embrace a new architectural style, known as the Gothic. Gothic structures, such as the Abbey Church of Saint-Denis in France and the rebuilt Canterbury Cathedral in England, have huge stained-glass windows, pointed vaults and arches (a technology developed in the Islamic world), and spires and flying buttresses. In contrast to heavy Romanesque buildings, Gothic architecture seems to be almost weightless.

Medieval religious art took other forms as well. Frescoes and mosaics decorated church interiors, and artists painted devotional images of the Virgin Mary, Jesus and the saints.

Also, before the invention of the printing press in the 15th century, even books were works of art. Craftsmen in monasteries (and later in universities) created illuminated manuscripts: handmade sacred and secular books with colored illustrations, gold and silver lettering and other adornments. In the 12th century, urban booksellers began to market smaller illuminated manuscripts, like books of hours, psalters and other prayer books, to wealthy individuals.

Economics And Society

In medieval Europe, rural life was governed by a system scholars call "feudalism."

In a feudal society, the king granted large pieces of land called fiefs to noblemen and bishops.

Landless peasants known as serfs did most of the work on the fiefs: They planted and harvested crops and gave most of the produce to the landowner. In exchange for their labor, they were allowed to live on the land. They were also promised protection in case of enemy invasion.

During the 11th century, however, feudal life began to change. Agricultural innovations such as the heavy plow and three-field crop rotation made farming more efficient and productive, so fewer farm workers were needed–but thanks to the expanded and improved food supply, the population grew.

As a result, more and more people were drawn to towns and cities.

Meanwhile, the Crusades had expanded trade routes to the East and given Europeans a taste for imported goods such as wine, olive oil and luxurious textiles.

As the commercial economy developed, port cities in particular thrived. By 1300, there were some 15 cities in Europe with a population of more than 50,000.

In these cities, a new era was born: the Renaissance. The Renaissance was a time of great intellectual and economic change, but it was not a complete "rebirth": It had its roots in the world of the Middle Ages.

The Silk Road – Ancient Trading Route Between Europe And Asia

The Silk Road is a name given to the many trade routes that connected Europe and the Mediterranean with the Asian world. The route is over 6,500 km long and got its name because the early Chinese traded silk along it.

Although silk was the main trading item there were many other goods that travelled along the Silk Road between Eastern Asia and Europe. In the course of time, medicine, perfumes, spicesand livestock found their way between continents.

The Chinese learned to make silk thousands of years ago. For a long time they were the only ones who knew how to make this preciousmaterial. Only the emperor, his family and his highest advisers were allowed to wear clothes made of silk. For a long time the Chinese guarded this secret very carefully.

The ancient Romans were the first Europeans who became aware of this wonderful material. Trading started, often with Indians as middlemen who traded silk with the Chinese in exchange for gold and silver which they got from the Romans.

Travelling along the route was dangerous. The hot desert, high mountains and sandstorms made travelling a rough business. Most of the goods along the Silk Road were carried by caravans.

44

Traders sometimes brought goods from one destination on the Silk Road to another, from where the goods would be transported by someone else.

Over the centuries people settled along the ancient route and many citiesemerged. Later on there were fewer hardships to overcome, but by no means was it easy.

Religion, languages and diseases also spread along the Silk Road. Buddhism, which originated in India, spread to China along this route. European traders probably brought the plague from Asia to Europe along the ancient road. In the early Middle Ages traffic along the route decreased because of the decline of the Roman Empire.

Trading along the Silk Road and became stronger again between the 13th and 14th centuries, when the Mongols controlled central Asia. During the Age of Exploration the Silk

Road lost its importance because new sea routes to Asia were discovered.

The Late Middle Ages

The Late Middle Ages or Late Medieval Period was the period of European history lasting from 1250 to 1500 AD. The Late Middle Ages followed the High Middle Ages and preceded the onset of the early modern period (and in much of Europe, the Renaissance).

Around 1300, centuries of prosperity and growth in Europe came to a halt. A series of famines and plagues, including the Great Famine of 1315–1317 and the Black Death, reduced the population to around half of what it was before the calamities.

Along with depopulation came social unrest and endemic warfare.

France and England experienced serious peasant uprisings, such as the Jac□uerie and the Peasants' Revolt, as well as over a century of intermittent conflict, the Hundred Years' War.

To add to the many problems of the period, the unity of the Catholic Church was temporarily shattered by the Western Schism. Collectively, those events are sometimes called the Crisis of the Late Middle Ages.

The Consecuences Of Reform

The conflicts between emperors and popes constituted one conspicuous result of the reform movement. The transformation and new institutionalization of learning, the reconstitution of the church, the intensification of ecclesiastical discipline, and the growth of territorial monarchies were four others. Each of these developments was supported by the agricultural, technological, and commercial expansion of the 10th and 11th centuries.

© *Prof. Manuel Freire-Garabal y Núñez*

The Transformation Of Thought And Learning

The polemics of the papal-imperial debate revealed the importance of establishing a set of canonical texts on the basis of which both sides could argue. A number of academic disciplines, particularly the study of dialectic, had developed considerably between the 9th and 12th centuries. By the 12th century it had become the most widely studied intellectual discipline, in part because it was an effective tool for constructing and refuting arguments.

The Gregorian reformers had also based their arguments on canon law, and a number of Gregorian and post-Gregorian collections, particularly that of Ivo of Chartres (c. 1040–1116), pointed the way toward the creation of a commonly accessible canon law.

That goal was achieved in about 1140–50 in two successive recensions (perhaps by two different authors) of a lawbook called Concordia discordantium canonum ("Concordance of Discordant Canons"), or Decretum, attributed to Master Gratian.

The Decretum became the standard introductory text of ecclesiastical law. Simultaneously, the full text of the 6th-century body of Roman law, later called the Corpus Iuris Civilis ("Body of Civil Law"), began to circulate in northern Italy and was taught in the schools of Bologna.

The learned character of the revived Roman law contributed powerfully to the development of legal science throughout Europe in the following centuries.

Early in the 12th century, Hugh of Saint-Victor (1096–1141), schoolmaster of a house of canons just outside Paris, wrote a description of all the subjects of learning, the Didascalicon.

Hugh's contemporary, Peter Abelard (1079–1142), taught dialectic at Paris to crowds of students, many of whom became high officials in ecclesiastical and secular institutions.

The teaching methods of scholars such as Gratian, Hugh, Abelard, and others became the foundation of Scholasticism, the method used by the new schools in the teaching of arts, law, medicine, and theology. In theologyitself, comparable canonical work was done by Peter Lombard (c. 1100–60) in his Sententiarum libri iv ("Four Books of Sentences"), which became, next to the Bible, the fundamental teaching text of theology.

But not all Christians admired the new Scholastic theology. The Scholastic teaching of Scripture replaced the early contemplative monastic style of exegesis with dialectical investigative techniques and speculative theology.

Many monks and some outraged laity thought that Scripture was being mishandled, stripped of its dignity and mystery in the service of feeble human logic and cold rationality.

They did not, however, stop the tide, as Scholastic theology created a complex, effective, and highly persuasive means of discussing both the complexities of divinity and the moral obligations of Christians on earth.

As groups of teachers organized themselves into guilds in the late 12th and early 13th centuries, they and their students received imperial, papal, and royal privileges.

About 1200 these associations, modeling themselves on ecclesiastical corporations, developed into the first universities.

During the remainder of the 13th century, clerical teaching authority within the universities was articulated.

The first guilds were formed for the teaching of law at several schools in Bologna and for the teaching of arts and theology at Paris and later at Oxford, Cambridge, and other towns. With the foundation of the University of Prague in 1348, the model crossed the Rhine River for the first time.

By the 15th century it had become a standard fixture of European learning.

University teachers insisted on the right to define teaching authority.

Proclaiming the earliest version of academic freedom, they rejected outside interference and asserted that their professional competence alone entitled them to determine the content of disciplines and the standards for admitting, examining, graduating, and certifying students.

They also transformed both the written script and the nature of the material book. Since teaching required a readable script and books whose texts were as close to identical as possible, the distinctive "Gothic" or "black letter" script was developed, which standardized abbreviations and the writing style used in texts.

The presence of universities of teachers and students in western European society was significant in itself.

The universities reflected favourably on the cities in which they were located and on the rulers who protected them.

The rulers also benefited from the opportunity to recruit increasingly educated public servants and bureaucrats from these institutions. The church benefited too, since the universities produced theologians, canon lawyers, and other officials that the church — even the papal office — now seemed to re□uire.

The universities aided in the recovery and dissemination of Aristotelianism, particularly in the physical sciences and metaphysics.

Only the new universities, moreover, could have housed and spread the intellectual work of Thomas Aquinas (1224/25–1274) and Bonaventure (1217–74), the greatest theologians of the 13th century, and of Henry of Segusio (Hostiensis; c. 1200–71) and Sinibaldo Fieschi (later Pope Innocent IV, reigned 1243–54), the greatest canon lawyers of the century.

Christianity, Judaism, And Islam

The sacred texts of revealed religions may be eternal and unchanging, but they are understood and applied by human beings living in time.

Christians believed not only that the Jews had misunderstood Scripture, thus justifying the

Christian reinterpretation of Jewish Scripture, but that all of Jewish Scripture had to be understood as containing only partial truth.

The whole truth was comprehensible only when Jewish Scripture was interpreted correctly, in what Christians called a "spiritual" rather than merely a "carnal" manner.

Although early Christian texts and later papal commands had prohibited the persecution and forced conversion of Jews, these doctrines were less carefully observed starting in the 11th century.

Heralded by a series of pogroms in both Europe and the Middle East carried out in the course of the First Crusade, a deeper and more widespread anti-Judaism came to characterize much of European history after 1100.

There also emerged in this period what some historians have termed "chimeric" anti-

Judaism, the conception of the Jew not only as ignorant of spiritual truth and stubbornly resistant to Christian preaching but as actively hostile to Christianity and guilty of ugly crimes against it, such as the ritual murder of Christian children and the desecration of the consecrated host of the mass.

This form of anti-Judaism resulted in massacres of Jews, usually at moments of high social tension within Christian communities.

One of the best documented of these massacres took place at York, Eng., in 1190.

Before the 11th century the Jews faced little persecution, lived among Christians, and even pursued the same occupations as Christians.

The Jews' restricted status after that time encouraged many of them to turn to moneylending, which only served to increase

Christian hostility (Christians were forbidden to lend money to other Christians).

Because the Jews often undertook on behalf of rulers work that Christians would not do or were not encouraged to do, such as serving as physicians and financial officers, Jews were hated both for their religion and for their social roles.

Jewish identity was also visually marked. Jews were depicted in particular ways in art, and the fourth Lateran Council in 1215 insisted that Jews wear identifying marks on their clothing.

 Even when not savagely persecuted, Jews were considered the property of the territorial monarchs of Europe and could be routinely exploited economically and even expelled, as they were from England in 1290, France in 1306, and Spain in 1492.

Yet Christians also believed that it was necessary for the Jews to continue to exist unconverted, because the Apocalypse, or Revelation to John, the last book of the Christian Bible, stated that the Jews would be converted at the end of time.

Therefore, a "saving remnant" of Jews needed to exist so that scriptural prophecy would be fulfilled.

Muslims, on the other hand, possessed neither the historical status of Jews nor their place in salvation history (the course of events from Creation to the Last Judgment).

To many Christian thinkers, Muslims were former Christian heretics who worshipped Muhammad, the Prophet of Islam, and were guilty of occupying the Holy Land and threatening Christendom with military force.

The First Crusade had been launched to liberate the Holy Land from Islamic rule, and later Crusades were undertaken to defend the original conquest.

The Crusading movement failed for many reasons but mainly because the material re□uirements for sustaining a military and political outpost so far from the heartland of western Europe were not met.

But as a component of European culture, the Crusade ideal remained prominent, even in the 15th and 16th centuries, when the powerful Ottoman Empire indeed threatened to sweep over Mediterranean and southeastern Europe.

Not until the Treaty of Carlowitz in 1699 was a stable frontier between the Ottoman Empire and the Holy Roman Empire established.

Contempt for Islam and fear of Muslim military power did not, however, prevent a lively and expansive commercial and technological transfer between the two civilizations or between them and the Byzantine Empire.

Commercial and intellectual exchanges between Islamic lands and western Europe were considerable.

Muslim maritime, agricultural, and technological innovations, as well as much East Asian technology via the Muslim world, made their way to western Europe in one of the largest technology transfers in world history.

What Europeans did not invent they readily borrowed and adapted for their own use. Of the three great civilizations of western Eurasia and North Africa, that of Christian Europe began as the least developed in virtually all aspects of material and intellectual culture, well behind the Islamic states and Byzantium.

By the end of the 13th century it had begun to pull even, and by the end of the 15th century it had surpassed both.

The late 15th-century voyages of discovery were not something new but a more ambitious continuation of the European interest in distant parts of the world.

From Territorial Principalities To Territorial Monarchies

As a result of the Investiture Controversy of the late 11th and early 12th centuries, the office of emperor lost much of its religious character and retained only a nominal universal preeminence over other rulers, though several 12th- and 13th-century emperors reasserted their authority on the basis of their interpretation of Roman law and energetically applied their lordship and pursued their dynastic interests in Germany and northern Italy.

But the struggle over investiture and the reform movement also legitimized all secular authorities, partly on the grounds of their obligation to enforce discipline.

The most successful rulers of the 12th and 13th centuries were, first, individual lords who created compact and more intensely governed principalities and, second and most important and enduring, kings who successfully asserted their authority over the princes, often with princely cooperation.

The monarchies of England, France, León-Castile, Aragon, Scandinavia, Portugal, and elsewhere all ac□uired their fundamental shape and character in the 12th century.

© *Prof. Manuel Freire-Garabal y Núñez*

The Office And Person Of The King

By the 12th century, most European political thinkers agreed that monarchy was the ideal form of governance, since it imitated on earth the model set by God for the universe.

It was also the form of government of the ancient Hebrews, the Roman Empire, and the peoples who succeeded Rome after the 4th century. For several centuries, some areas had no monarch, but these were regarded as anomalies. Iceland (until its absorption by Norway in 1262) was governed by an association of free men and heads of households meeting in an annual assembly.

Many city-republics in northern Italy—especially Florence, Milan, Genoa, Pisa, and Venice—were in effect independent from the 10th to the 16th century, though they were nominally under the rule of the emperor.

© *Prof. Manuel Freire-Garabal y Núñez*

Elsewhere in Europe, the prosperous and volatile cities of the Low Countries fre⬜uently asserted considerable independence from the counts of Flanders and the dukes of Brabant. In the 15th century the forest cantons of Switzerland won effective independence from their episcopal and lay masters.

For the rest of Europe, however, monarchy was both a theoretical norm and a factual reality.

Whereas kings were originally rulers of peoples, from the 11th century they gradually became rulers of peoples in geographic territories, and kingdoms came to designate both ruled peoples and the lands they inhabited. Gradually, inventories of royal resources, royal legislation, and the idea of borders and territorial maps became components of territorial monarchies.

Kings acquired their thrones by inheritance, by election or acclamation (as in the empire), or by conquest.

The first two means were considered the most legitimate, unless conquest was carried out at the request or command of a legitimate authority, usually the pope.

The king's position was confirmed by a coronation ceremony, which acknowledged what royal blood claimed: a dynastic right to the throne, borne by a family rather than a designated individual.

Inheritance of the throne might involve the successor's being designated coruler while the previous king still lived (as in France), designation by the will of the predecessor, or simply agreement and acclamation by the most important and powerful royal subjects.

When dynasties died out in the male line, the search for a ruler became more complicated; when they died out in the male line and a woman succeeded, there were usually intense debates about the legitimacy of female succession.

Liturgical anointing with consecrated oil was accompanied by the ceremonial presentation to the king of objects with symbolic meaning (the crown, the sword of justice, and the helmet, robe, and scepter), by the chanting of prayers dedicated to rulership, and usually by an oath, in which the king swore to protect the church, the weak, and the peace of his kingdom, to administer justice, and to defend the kingdom against its (and his) enemies.

From the very beginning of European history, kings had responsibilities as well as rights and powers. Kings who were thought to have violated their oaths might be considered tyrants or incompetents, and a number of kings were deposed by local factions or papal command, especially in the 13th and 14th centuries. Depositions also required ceremonies that reversed the coronation liturgy.

Instruments Of Royal Governance

Kings ruled through their courts, which were gradually transformed from private households into elaborate bureaucracies.

Royal religious needs were served by royal chapels—whose personnel often became bishops in the kingdom—and by clerical chancellors, who were responsible for issuing and sealing royal documents.

Royal chanceries, financial offices, and law courts became specialized institutions during the 12th century.

They recruited people of skill as well as of respectable birth, and they established programs to ensure uniformity and norms of professional competence, goals that were increasingly aided by the education offered by the new universities.

In some circumstances, kings were expected to seek and follow the advice of the most important men in their kingdoms, and these gatherings were formalized after the 12th century.

Kings also sometimes convened larger assemblies of lower-ranking subjects in order to issue their commands or urge approval of financial demands. As kings grew stronger and their bureaucracies more articulated, their costs, particularly for war, also increased.

Greater financial needs often determined a king's use of representative institutions in order to gain widespread acceptance of new direct or indirect taxation.

These assemblies developed differently in different kingdoms. In England the first Parliamentswere held in the late 13th century, though they were not powerful institutions until the 16th century.

In France the Parlement developed into a royal law court, while the intermittentmeetings of the Estates-General (a representative assembly of the three orders of society) served as an instrument of consultation and communication for the kings. Across Europe these representative assemblies were composed differently, functioned differently, and possessed different degrees of influence on the ruler and the rest of the kingdom. Their later role as essential and powerful components of government began only in the 16th and 17th centuries.

The territorial monarchies represented something entirely new in world history.

Although they often borrowed from the political literature of anti□uity-—from the Greek philosopher Aristotle, the Roman statesman Cicero, and Roman epic poetry— they applied it to a very different world, one whose ideas were shaped by courtiers, professors, and canon lawyers as well as by political philosophers.

Incorporating both clergy and laity under vigorous royal dynasties, the kingdoms of Europe grew out of the political experience of the papacy, the north Italian city-republics, and their own internal development.

By the 15th century the territorial monarchies had laid the groundwork for the modern state.

When, to further their own interests, they began to incorporate successively lower levels of society, they also laid the groundwork for the nation. The combination of these, the nation-state, became the characteristic form of the early modern European and Atlantic polity.

The Three Orders

In the 11th and 12th centuries thinkers argued that human society consisted of three orders: those who fight, those who pray, and those who labour.

The structure of the second order, the clergy, was in place by 1200 and remained intact until the religious reformations of the 16th century.

The very general category of those who labour (specifically, those who were not knightly warriors or nobles) diversified rapidly after the 11th century into the lively and energetic worlds of peasants, skilled artisans, merchants, financiers, lay professionals, and

© *Prof. Manuel Freire-Garabal y Núñez*

entrepreneurs, which together drove the European economy to its greatest achievements. The first order, those who fight, was the rank of the politically powerful, ambitious, and dangerous. Kings took pains to ensure that it did not resist their authority.

The term noble was originally used to refer to members of kinship groups whose names and heroic past were known, respected, and recognized by others (though it was not usually used by members of such groups themselves).

Noble groups married into each other, recognizing the importance of both the female and the male lines.

Charlemagne used this international nobility to rule his empire, and its descendants became the nobility of the 11th and 12th centuries, though by then the understanding of noble status had changed.

During the 11th century, however, some branches of these broad groups began to identify themselves increasingly with the paternal line and based their identity on their possession of a particular territory handed down from generation to generation, forming patriarchal lineages whose consciousness of themselves differed from that of their predecessors. Titles such as count or duke were originally those of royal service and might increase the prestige and wealth of a family but were not originally essential to noble status.

Nor were even kings thought to be able to ennoble someone who was not noble by birth.

As the status of the free peasant population was diminished, freedom and unfreedom, as noted above, gradually became the most significant social division (see above Demographic and agricultural growth).

The new warrior order encompassed both great nobles and lesser fighting men who depended upon the great nobles for support.

This assistance usually took the form of land or income drawn from the lord's resources, which could also bring the hope of social advancement, even marriage into a lordly family.

The acute need on the part of these lower-ranking warriors was to distinguish themselves from peasants — hence the relegation of all who were not warriors to the vague category of those who labour.

Some nobles asserted their nobility by seizing territory, controlling it and its inhabitants from a castle, surviving as local powers over several generations, marrying well, achieving recognition from their neighbours, and dispensing ecclesiastical patronage to nearby monasteries.

The greatest and wealthiest of the nobles controlled vast areas of land, which they received by inheritance or through a grant from the king.

Some of them developed closely governed territorial principalities which, in France, were eventually absorbed and redistributed by the crown to members of the royal family or their favourites.

Despite the extreme diversity between knights, lesser nobility, and greater nobility, their common warrior-culture, expressed in the literature and ideology of chivalry, served as an effective social bond, excluding all those who did not share it.

As the territorial monarchies gradually increased in both prestige and power, the higher nobility adjusted by accepting more royal offices, titles, and patronage, developing an elaborate vocabulary of noble status, and restricting access to its ranks even though kings could now ennoble whomever they chose.

The culture of chivalry served the ambitions of the lower-ranking nobility, but it also reflected the spectrum of different levels of nobility, all subordinated to the ruler.

The culture and power of the European aristocracy lasted until the end of the 18th century.

Crisis, Recovery, And Resilience

Both ancient and modern historians have often conceived the existence of civilizations and historical periods in terms of the biological stages of human life: birth, development, maturity, and decay.

Once the Middle Ages was identified as a distinct historical period, historians in the 15th and 16th centuries began to describe it as enduring in a sequence of stages from youthful vigour to maturity (in the 12th and 13th centuries) and then sinking into old age (in the 14th and 15th centuries).

Much of the evidence used to support this view was based on the series of apparently great disasters that struck Europe in the 14th century: the Mongol invasions, the great famine of 1315, the Black Death of 1348 and subsequent years, the financial collapse of the great Italian banking houses in the early 14th century, and the vastly increased costs and devastating effects of larger-scale warfare.

For a long time historians considered these disasters dramatic signs of the end of an age, especially because they already believed that the Renaissance had emerged following the collapse of medieval civilization.

Despite the crises, the 14th century was also a time of great progress in the arts and sciences. Following a renewed interest in ancient Greek and Roman texts that took root in the High Middle Ages, the Italian Renaissance began.

The absorption of Latin texts had started before the Renaissance of the 12th centurythrough contact with Arabs during the Crusades, but the availability of important Greek texts accelerated with the Capture of Constantinople by the Ottoman Turks, when many Byzantine scholars had to seek refuge in the West, particularly Italy.

Combined with this influx of classical ideas was the invention of printing, which facilitated dissemination of the printed word and democratized learning. Those two things would later lead to the Protestant Reformation. Toward the end of the period, the Age of Discovery began. The expansion of the

Ottoman Empire cut off trading possibilities with the East.

Europeans were forced to seek new trading routes, leading to the Spanish expedition under Christopher Columbus to the Americas in 1492 and Vasco da Gama's voyage to Africa and India in 1498. Their discoveries strengthened the economy and power of European nations.

The changes brought about by these developments have led many scholars to view this period as the end of the Middle Ages and the beginning of modern history and of early modern Europe.

However, the division is somewhat artificial, since ancient learning was never entirely absent from European society.

As a result, there was developmental continuity between the ancient age (via classical antiquity) and the modern age. Some historians, particularly in Italy, prefer not to speak of the Late Middle Ages at all but rather see the high period of the Middle Ages transitioning to the Renaissance and the modern era.

The Twentieth Century And Beyond

It would have been hard to imagine a 20th century in which international law had not evolved and expanded, yet the century turned out to be rather more eventful, to use a neutral term, than could have been prophesied at its beginning.

Following incomprehensible tragedies infl icted by Man upon its own kind, international law was left bereft of lofty aspirations; but suffering and decay also came to colour the background against which new treaties, new procedures, and new institutions emerged as civilization gained ground anew.

Civilizing impetus joined forces with rather more mundane causes of treaty-making, such as increase in trans-border activities, technological innovation, greater appetite for regulation worldwide, and mere coincidence.

In political terms, the 20th century brought about a gradual transfer of power from Europe, "a forest of symbols" , to what had until then been the peripheries, in particular the United States. In the fi rst half of the century, infl uential ideas about international law were promoted by American statesmen in European cities such as The Hague and Paris.

The names of Elihu Root, Woodrow Wilson, and Francis B. Kellogg come to mind, among others. Many of those ideas – a permanent court of international justice, a general association of nations, and renunciation of war – were taken further when establishing the United Nations Organization in the aftermath of the Second World War, the key defi ning event of the century.

Principles of individual criminal responsibility were articulated by the International Military Tribunal at Nuremberg, the establishment of which had been preceded by clashes between

© *Prof. Manuel Freire-Garabal y Núñez*

traditions and policies. Even in the waning moments of the Second World War the United States Government had been sunk in controversy over what to do with the major war criminals of the European Axis.

The British Government was disposed, on balance, to subject enemy leaders to a ⬜uick despatch before a fi ring squad, whereas the proposal of the Soviet Government to have a trial blended in with the dark shadows of the Great Terror's show trials.

The road to Nuremberg was cleared only once President Roosevelt had been succeeded by Henry S. Truman, once a county judge.

While in the second half of the century the West and the East fought out the Cold War yet another former periphery, the South, fathered a breed of new, albeit vulnerable, states in the process of decolonization sanctioned by legal principle, i.e., the right of peoples to self-

© *Prof. Manuel Freire-Garabal y Núñez*

determination. It contributed to an increase in the membership of the United Nations from 51 to 192.

In Europe, the legacy of the Second World War rested also in the European Convention on Human Rights with its supervisory mechanism, notably the European Court of Human Rights, and the European Communities, the first international organization to be rooted in the rule of law under the auspices of the European Court of Justice.

The Cold War ended without the remaining international political structures and their legal bases having suffered ignominy to the point of futility.

But on a smaller scale, many a European (and also many others) found the time ripe for new ideas of internationalism to be introduced in Washington, DC, with the International Criminal Court and a so-called war on

© *Prof. Manuel Freire-Garabal y Núñez*

terrorism as prominent recent venues for clashes between moralism and Realpolitik.

In the same 20th century, a craving for literate battles anchored in jurisprudence, if not philosophy, gave way for international law as a legal discipline concerned with the practical application of law to specifi c cases.

The signifi cance of the transformation from theory to practice is thrown into relief by the High Court of Admiralty's classic dictum depicting Hugo Grotius and his infl uence: "pedantic man in his closet dictates the law of nations; everybody quotes, and nobody minds him".

After all, when in the late 19th century a Cambridge professor preparing his lectures on international law for publication received an invitation for further studies of Grotius in a friend's.

Civil Law & Common Law

In comparative law, there are many situations where the same legal term has different meanings, or where different legal terms have same legal effect.

This can often cause confusion to both lawyers and their clients. This confusion most often occurs when civil lawyers have to deal with common law, or aice aersa, when common law lawyers deal with civil law issues. While there are many issues which are dealt with in the same way by the civil law and common law systems, there remain also significant differences between these two legal systems related to legal structure, classification, fundamental concepts, terminology, etc.

© *Prof. Manuel Freire-Garabal y Núñez*

Notion Of Civil Law

Civil law has its origin in Roman law, as codified in the Corpus Iuris Civilis of Justinian. Under this influence, in the ensuing period the civil law has been developed in Continental Europe and in many other parts of the world.

The main feature of civil law is that it is contained in civil codes/ which are described as a "systematic, authoritative, and guiding statute of broad coverage, breathing the spirit of reform and marking a new start in the legal life of an entire nation."

Most civil codes were adopted in the nineteenth and twentieth centuries: French Code Civil, 1804, Austrian Biirgerliches Gesetzbuch, 1811, German Biirgerliches Gesetzbuch, 1896, Japanese Minpo, 1896, Swiss Zivilgesetzbuch, 1907, Italian Codice Civile, 1942, etc.

Between these codes there are some important differ-ences, and they are often grouped in the Romanic and the Germanic families.

Even though the civil codes of different countries are not homogenous, there are certain features of all civil codes which bind them together and "sets them apart from those who practice under different systems."

Civil law is largely classified and structured and contains a great number of general rules and principles, often lacking details.

One of the basic characteris¬tics of the civil law is that the courts main task is to apply and interpret the law contained in a code, or a statute to case facts.

The assumption is that the code regulates all cases that could occur in practice, and when certain cases are not regulated by the code, the

© *Prof. Manuel Freire-Garabal y Núñez*

courts should apply some of the general principles used to fill the gaps.

Notion Of Common Law

Common law evolved in England since around the 11th century and was later adopted in the USA, Canada, Australia, New Zealand and other countries of the British Commonwealth.

The most obvious distinction between civil law and common law systems is that a civil law system is a codified system, where¬as the common law is not created by means of legislation but is based mainly on case law.

The principle is that earlier judicial decisions, usually of the higher courts, made in a similar case, should be followed in the subse☐uent cases, i.e. that precedents should be respected. This principle is known as stare decisis and has never been legislated but is regarded as binding by the courts, which can even decide to modify it.?

The claim that common law is created by the case law is only partly true, as the common law is based in large part on statutes, which the ludges are supposed to apply and interpret in much the same way as the judges in civil law (e.g. the Sale of Coods Act,7979, the Uniform Commercial Code, etc.).

Comparison Between Civil Law And Common Law

The common law and civil law systems are the products of two fundamen¬tally different approaches to the legal process.

In civil law, the main principles and rules are contained in codes and statutes, which are applied by the courts codes.

Hence, codes and statutes prevail, while case law constitutes only a sec¬ondary source of law.

On the other hand, in the common law system, the law has been dominantly created by judicial decisions, while a conceptual structure is often lacking.

This difference is the result of different role of legislator in civil law and common law. The civil law is based on the theory of separation of pow¬ers, whereby the role of legislator is to legislate, while the courts should apply the law.

On the other hand, in common law the courts are given the main task in creating the law.

The civil law is based on codes which contain logically connected concepts and rules, starting with general principles and moving on to specific rules.

A civil lawyer usually starts from a legal norm contained in a legislation, and by means of deduction makes conclusions regarding the actual case.

On the other hand, a lawyer in common law starts with the actual case and compares it with the same or similar legal issues that have been dealt with by courts in previous¬ly decided cases, and from these relevant precedents the binding legal rule is determined by means of induction.

A consequence of this fundamental differ¬ence between the two systems is that lawyers from the civil law countries tend to be more conceptual, while lawyers from the common law countries are con¬sidered to be more pragmatic.

One of the main differences between the civil law and common law systems is the binding force of precedents.

© *Prof. Manuel Freire-Garabal y Núñez*

While the courts in the civil law system have as their main task deciding particular cases by applying and interpreting legal norms, in the common law the courts are supposed not only to decide disputes between particular parties but also to provide guidance as to how similar dis putes should be settled in the future.

The interpretation of a legislation given by a court in specific case is binding on lower courts, so that under common law the court decisions still make the basis for interpretation of legislation.

On the other hand, in contrast to common law, the case law in civil law sys¬tems does not have binding force.

The doctrine of stare decisis does not apply to civil law courts, so that court decisions are not binding on lower courts in subsequent cases, nor are they binding on the same courts, and it is not uncommon for courts to reach opposite conclusions in similar cases.

In civil law the courts have the task to interpret the law as contained in a legislation, without being bound by the interpretation of the same legislation given by higher courts; this means that under civil law the courts do not create the law, but only apply and interpret it.

In practice, however, the higher court decisions certainly have a certain influence on lower courts, since judges of lower courts will usually take into account the risk that their decisions would probably be reversed by the higher court if they contradict the higher court decisions. Judges normally try to avoid the reversal of their decisions by higher courts as if too many of their decisions are reversed their promotion may be adversely affected.

Hence, even though in civil law systems the case law formally has no binding force, it is

© *Prof. Manuel Freire-Garabal y Núñez*

generally recognized that courts should take into account prior decisions, especially when the settled case law shows that a line of cases has developed.

Bibliography

The following list is confined to the most useful and readily obtainable books which should be found in any good public library.

1. Eg.. Sir John Fortcscuc. The Governance of England, C Plummer, ed. (Oxford. 1885) 14-32; H.M. Cam. 'The Decline and Fall of English Feudalism. Liberties and Communities in Medieval England.' 213-14. rpt. from History, n.s. 25 (1940 I) 216 33; J.G Bellamy. Crime and Public Order in England in the later Middle Ages < London. 1973) esp ch I. BA Hanawalt, 'Fur Collar Crime.' Journal of Social History 8 (1975) 1-17; S.L Waugh. 'The Profits of Violence." Speculum 52 (1977) 843-69,

2. See especially K.B. McFarlane, 'Bastard Feudalism,' Bulletin of the Institute of Historical Research 20 (1945) 161 80. 'The

Wars of the Roses.' Proceedings of the British Academy 50 (1964) 87-119. both in G.L. Hamss. cd.. Collected Essays (London. I98l)and Hamss's introduction, xix-xx. McFarlane. *Service. Maintenance and Politics.' Ihe Mobility of later Medieval England (Oxford, 1973) 120-21. The author would here like lo record her profound debt to the works of McFarlane, apparent throughout the article, for their unrivalled understanding and insight into the period, much of which has yet to be absorbed

3. M.T Clanchy, 'Law. Government and Society in Medieval England.' History 59 (1974) 73 78; G.L. liarriss. Introduction to McFarlanet Collected Essays, supra note 2.

4. See works cited in supra note I See also. e g .R.A Griffiths. Ihe Reign of King Henry VI (London, 1981) 130-38. 595-97; C. Ross. Edward IV (London. 1974) 388-413; J.R. Lander. Conflict and Stability in Fifteenth'Century England. 3d cd (London, 1977) 164-68. J.T. Rosenthal, Nobles and the Noble Life (London, 1976) 81-88, A Harding. 'Early Trailbaston Proceedings,* in R.F. Hunnisett and J.B Post, eds.. Medieval Legal Records edited in Memory of C.A. F. Meekmgs (London. 1978) 150 51; R. L. Storey. The End of the House of Lancaster! London, 1966)10 17. Thequotation is from Clanchy, 'Law. Government and Society.* supra note 3. 75.

5. Aegean Civilization and the Greeks before the Persian Wars. Botsford, Hellenic History, chaps, i—ix.

WESTERMANN, Ancient Nations, pp. 43-50, chaps, vii-x. GOODSPEED, Ancient World. Breasted, Ancient Times, chaps, viii- xii. My RES, Dawn of History, chaps, viii-ix. Kkinach, Story of Art, pp. 26-32. IIawes, Crete the Forerunner of Greece. B.AIKIK, Sea Kings of Crete. IIOGARTIl, The /Indent East. MOSSO, Daunt of Mediterranean Civilization. IIall, Ancient History of the .Year East, pp. 31-72. ZlMMRRN, Greek Commonwealth (second edition). Greenidge, Greek Constitutional History. Capps, Homer to Theocritus. Kf.I.I.ER, Homeric Life. SEYMOUR, Homeric Age. SANDYS, Companion to Greek Studies. MAIIAFFY, Social Life in Greece.

6. The Persian Wars and the Age of Pericles. Botsford, Hellenic History. NVestermann, Ancient Nations, chaps,

xi-xvii. Goodspked, Ancient World. Breasted, Ancient Times, chaps, xiii-xviii. Abbott, Pericles. Hall, Near East. chap. xii. GRUNDY, Great Persian War. SEIGNOBOS, Ancient Civilization. Grant, Greece in the Age of Pericles. ZlMMERN, Greek Commonwealth. Sandys, Companion. TARBELL, History of Greek Art. MUNROK, History of Elucation. Ferguson, Greek Imperialism. .

7. The Roman Empire and its Decline. Hotsford. History of home, w estf.r-mann, Ancient Nations. GoonsrF.F.D, Ancient World. BREASTED, Ancient Times, chaps, xxvii-xxix. Fowi.er, Rome. Cafes. Early Empire. Jones. Roman Empire. BURY. Students' Roman Empire, chaps, i-xii. Abbott. Roman Political Institutions, chap. xii. Davis. Influence of Wealth. Firth, Augustus.

8. Fowler, History of Roman Literature, Bk. II. MaCKAIL, Roman Literature, Bk. II. TUCKER, Life in the Roman World. ARNOLD, Roman Provincial Administration. KEINACH, Story of Art, pp. 75-83. PELLISON, Roman Life in Pliny's Time. MaU and Kelsey, Pomfei. Tucker, Roman Life, chaps, i-iii, xix-xxi. Hardy, Studies in Roman History, Series I. Cumont, Oriental Religions in Roman Paganism. Gl.OVKR, Conflict of Religions in the Roman Empire. Oman, Pyzantine Empire. Cottf.rill, Mediarval Italy, pp. 21-54. FlRTH. Constantine. Dill, Roman Society in the ImsI Century of the Roman Empire.

9. Rise of the Papacy ; the Monks. Thorndike, History of Medieval Europe, chap, vi, ix-x. Flick, The Rise of the Medieval Church. Walker, The History

of the Christian Church. Church histories are usually written by either Catholics or Protestants, who naturally differ in their interpretation of events. One may refer to FlSIIER, History of the Christian Church (Protestant), or ALZOG, Manual of Universal Church History (Catholic). Milma.n, History of luitin Christianity. Cambridge Medieval History, Vol. I, chaps, iv, vi. Newman, Manual of Church History, Vol. I (Protestant). Workman, Evolution of the Monastic Ideal. Taylor, Henry O., Classical Heritage of the Middle Ages, admirable chapter on Monasticism. Harnack, Monastic ism. Cambridge Medieval History, Vol. II, chap. xvi.

10. Mohammed and his Followers. For Mohammed and the Saracens, see Thatcher and Schwill, Europe in the Middle Age, chap. xv. Gilman, The

Saracens. GIBBON has a famous chapter on Mohammed and another on the conquests of the Arabs. These arc the fiftieth and fifty-first of his great work. Cambridge Medieval History, Vol. II, chaps, x-xii. MUIR, Life of Mohammed. Ameer ALI, The Life and Teachings of Mohammed, a Short History of the Saracens, by one who sympathizes with them. It is not hard to find a copy of one of the English translations of the Koran. Sec brief extracts in Robinson, Readings, and in Ogg, Source Booh of Mediaval History, pp. 97 ff. STANLEY Lane-Poole, Speeches and Table Talk of Mohammed, is very interesting.

11. The Medieval Church; Heresy and the Friars. Emerton, Medieval Europe, chap. xvi. The works of Flick and Walker referred to above are useful brief treatments. Special topics can be looked

up in the Encyclopedia Britan- nica, the Catholic Encyclopedia, or any other good encyclopedia. Cutts, Parish Priests and their People. Lea, A Histosy of the Inquisition of the Middle Ages, contains chapters upon the origin of both the Franciscan and Dominican orders. For St. Francis the best work is Sabatier, St. Francis of Assisi. See also Gasquet, English Monastic Life', J ESSOPP, The Coming of the Friars, and Other Historic Essays; CREIGHTON, History of the Papacy, introductory chapter.

12. Europe at the Opening of the Sixteenth Century. IIayf.s. C. J. H., Political and Social History of Modem Europe, Vol. I, chaps, i, iii (excellent brief account). Johnson, Europe in the Sixteenth Century, chaps, i-ii. Cambridge Modem History, Vol. I, chaps, iv, xi. See " Charles V," in Encyclopedia Britan- nica.

DURUY, History of France, Ninth and Tenth Periods.

13. Cambridge Modem History, Vol. II, chap. ii. Dyer and IlASSALL, Modem Europe (a political history of Europe in 6 vols.), Vol. I. Creighton, History of the Papaey. Pastor, History of the Popes, Vol. V. Bryce, Holy Roman Empire, chap. xiv.

14. The Wars of Religion. Johnson, Europe in the Sixteenth Century, chaps, vii-ix. Hayes, Modem Europe, Vol. I, chaps, v-vi (excellent). Wakeman, European History, ijqS-iyij, chaps, i-v. The portion of the chapter dealing with English affairs can be readily supplemented by means of the general histories of England, Chbyney, Cross, Green, Gardiner, Terry, etc.

15. Cambridge Meuiem History, Vol. II, chaps, ix, xvi, xviii-xix ; Vol. Ill, chaps, i, vi-x, xv, xx; Vol. IV, chaps, i, iii-vi, xiii-xiv. Lindsay, History of the Reformotion, Vol. II, Bk. Ill, chaps, iv-v, and Bk. VI. Putnam, Ruth, William the Silent. Payne, Voyages of Elizabethan Seamen to America, Vol. 1. MOTLEY, Rise of the Dutch Republic. GlNDELY, History of the Thirty Years' War.

16. Central and Eastern Europe. Cambridge Modem History, Vol. V, chaps, xvi, xx-xxi; Vol. VI. 11ENDERSON, A Short History of Germany, Vol. I. Ram baud, History 0/ Russia, Vols. I−II. Tuttle, History of Prussia (4 vols.). RriglIT, Maria Theresa. CARLYLE, History of Frederick the Second, called Frederick the Great, a classic. Evkrsley, The Partitions of Poland. HasSALL, The Balance of Power, 17/3-1789, full account of

diplomacy and wars. Kluchevsky, A History of Russia (3 vols.). PHILLIPS, Poland (Home University Series). ScilKVIl.I., The Making of Modem Germany, Lectures I—11. ScilUYi.KR, Peter the Great, standard English biography. WaLISZENVSKI, Life of Peter the Great.

17. Napoleon and Europe. Cambridge Modem History, VoL VIII, chaps, xviii-xxv; Vol. IX, chops. i-iii. Fisher, Napoleon (Home University Series), chaps, i-v. Fournier, Napoleon the First, chaps, i-vii, excellent. Johnston, Napoleon, chaps, i-vi, the best brief account in English. Rose, The Life of Napoleon the First, Vol. I, chaps, i-xi, the most scholarly account in English. Anderson, Constitutions and Other Seleet Documents Illustrative of the His-toy of France, /7S9-/907. BlNGHAM, A

Selection from the Letters and Despatches of the First Napoleon (3 vols.). I-AS Cases, The Journal of the Emperor Napoleon at St. Helena. LECESTRK, New Letters of Napoleon I. De R£musat. Memoirs of Madame de Rem usat. MIOT 1>E M ELITO, Memoirs of Miot de Melito. BIGELOW, A History of the German Struggle for Liberty. SEELEY, The Life and 7'inus of Stein, a study of Prussia under Stein. SLOANE, Life of Napoleon Bonaparte, Vols. 111-IV. 'Paine, The Modem Rfgime (2 vols.), keen analysis of Napoleon.

18. Revolutionary Europe – Italian and German Unity. In addition to the general histories cited above, there are the following special volumes: Cambridge Modem History, Vo). XI. Maurice, Revolutionary Movement of 1848- iS4g. Harry, The Papacy and Modern Times

(Home University Scries). Garibaldi, Autobiography. Mazzini, Duties of Man (Everyman's Library). Cesaresco, Cavour and the Liberation of Italy. King, A History of Italian Unity (2 vols.). STILLMAN, The Union of Italy. BlSMARCK, Bismarck, the Man and the Statesman, an autobiography. BUSCH, Bismarck, Some Secret Pages of his History. IIEADLAM, Bismarck and the Foundation of the German Umpire. Schevill, The Making of Modem Germany, Lectures I-V, very enthusiastic. Smith, Bismarck and German Unity. TrKITSCHKK, History of Germany in the Nineteenth Century, and Politics (2 vols.). GuiLLAND, Modem Germany and her Historians.

19. The British Empire. Cambridge Modern History, V'ol. XI, chap, xxvii; Vol. XII, chap. xx. CttEYNEY, A Short History of

England, chap. xx. Hazen, Europe since /S/J, chap. xxii. Oman, England in the Nineteenth Century, chaps, ix-xii. Story, The British Empire. BURINOT, Canada under British Buie. DlLKE, Problems of Creator Britain. EgertoN, A Short History of British Colonial Policy. Eraser, British Buie in India. HOBSON, The War in South Africa. I.N'NES, A History of England and the British Empire, Vol. IV. Jenks, A History of the Australasian Colonies. Lowell, The Government of England, Vol. II, chaps, liv-lviii. McCarthy, A History of Our Oxen Times (7 vols.), Vols. V-VII. Paul, A History of Modern England, Vols. II, IV. Source Material. Robinson and Beard, Readings, chap, xxvii.

www.ingramcontent.com/pod-product-compliance
Lightning Source LLC
Chambersburg PA
CBHW030344290526
45785CB00004B/1595